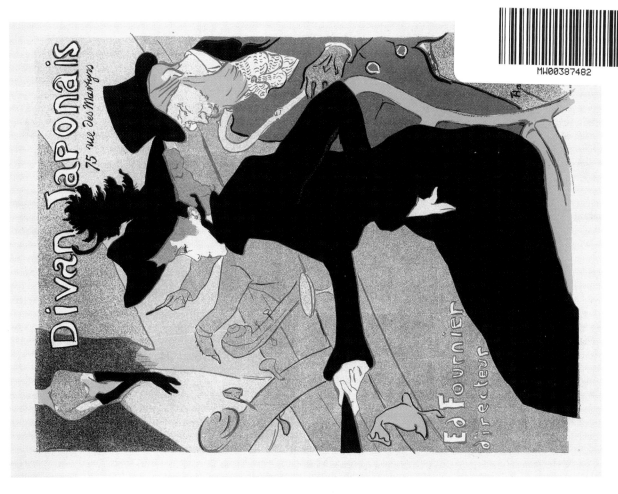

002. Henri de Toulouse-Lautrec

001. Jules Chéret

004. DUDLEY HARDY

003. JULIUS PRICE

006. LOUIS RHEAD

005. GEORGES MEUNIER

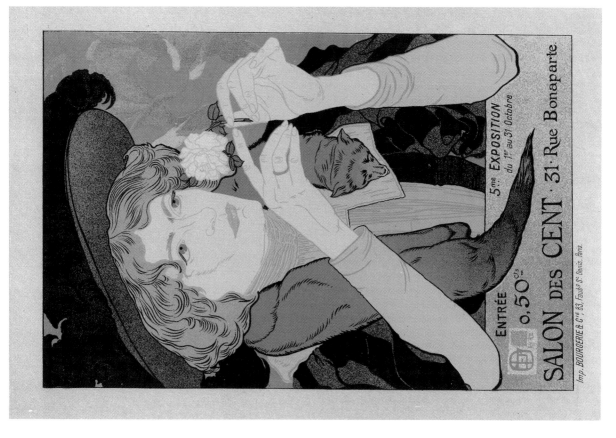

008. Georges de Feure

007. Jules Chéret

010. F.-A. CAZALS

009. LUCIEN LEFÉVRE

012. JULES CHÉRET

011. THE BEGGARSTAFFS

014. EDWARD PENFIELD

013. EUGÈNE GRASSET

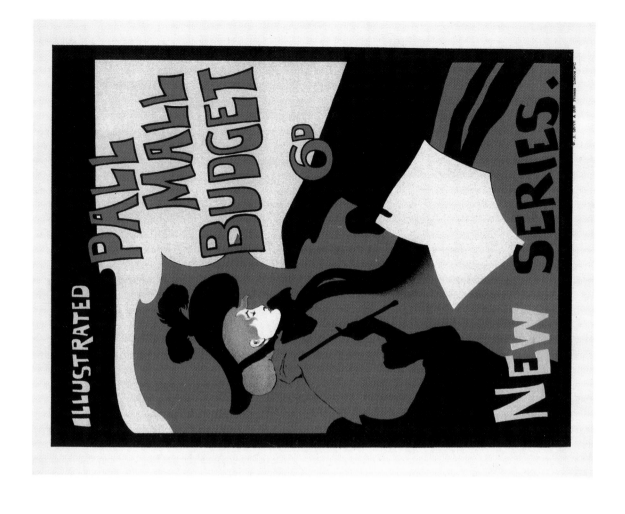

016. MAURICE GREIFFENHAGEN

015. LUCIEN MÉTIVET

017. Maurice Boutet de Monvel

018. Alphonse Maria Mucha

020. Albert Guillaume

019. Edouard Duyck and Adolphe Crespin

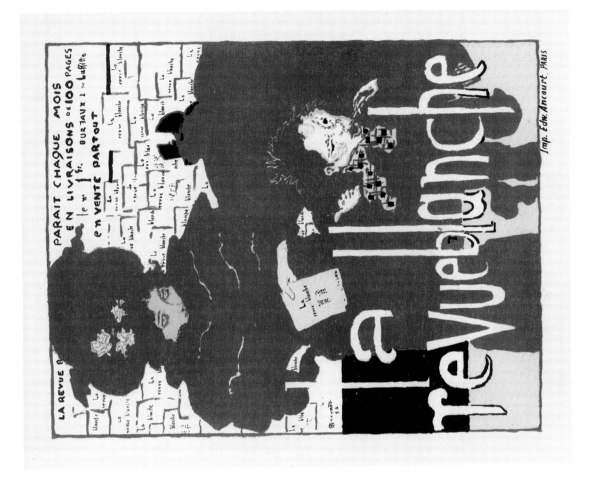

022. PIERRE BONNARD

021. JULES CHÉRET

024. Jules Chéret

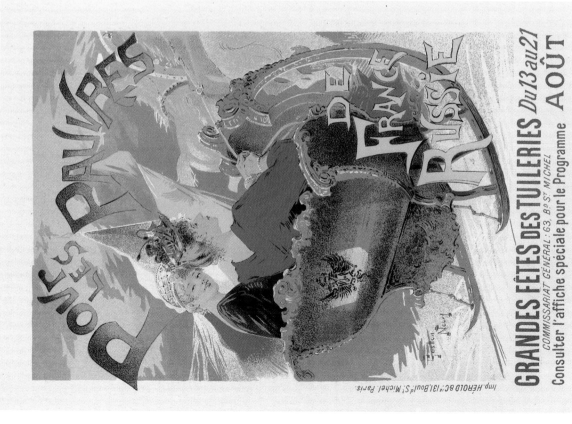

023. Gaston Noury

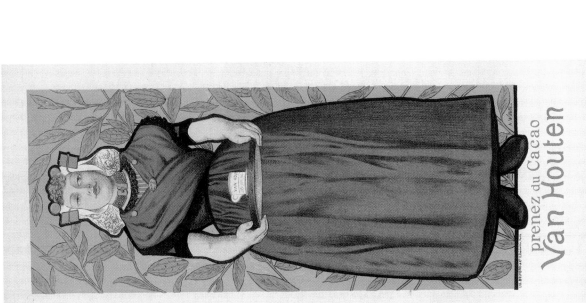

026. WILLIAM CARQUEVILLE

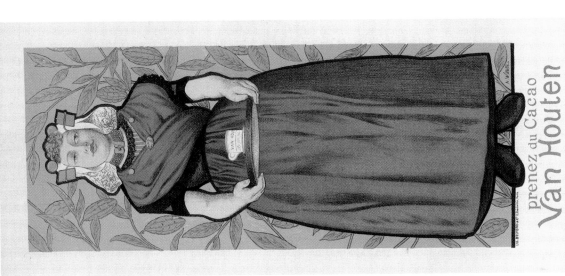

025. ADOLPHE WILLETTE

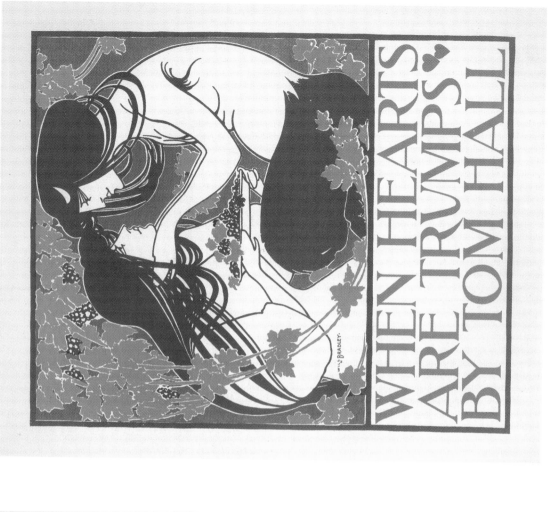

028. WILL BRADLEY

027. FIRMIN BOUISSET

030. Lucien Lefèvre

029. Jules Chéret

032. THE BEGGARSTAFFS

031. GEORGES MEUNIER

034. CARAN D'ACHE

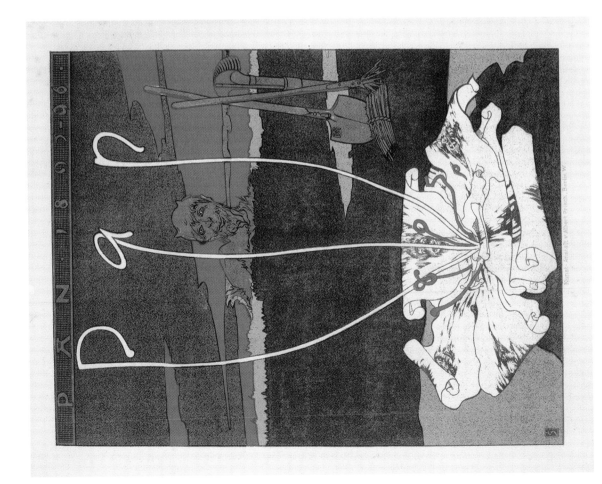

033. JOSEPH SATTLER

036. ROEDEL

035. JULES CHÉRET

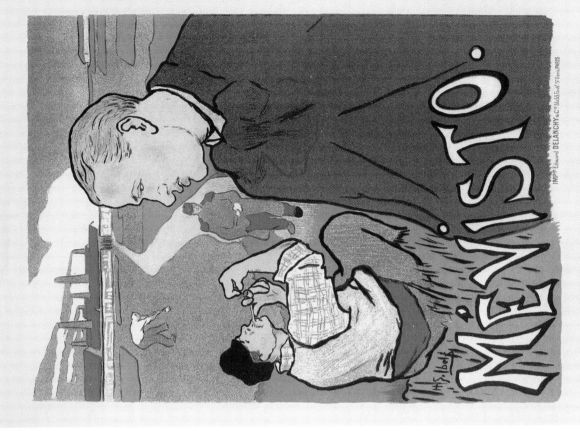

038. Henri-Gabriel Ibels

037. M. Louise Stowell

040. HENRI DE TOULOUSE-LAUTREC

039. ALBERT GEORGE MORROW

042. PAUL FISCHER

041. HENRI GERBAULT

045. Otto Fischer

046. Privat Livemont

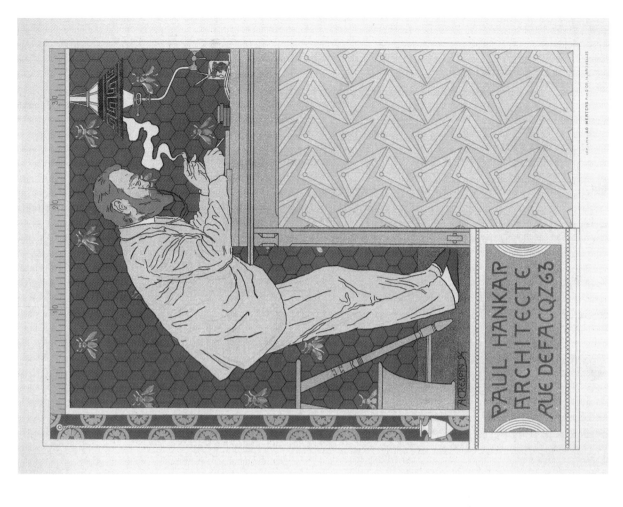

048. Adolphe Crespin

047. Lucien Lefèvre

050. Jules Chéret

049. Dudley Hardy

052. Théophile-Alexandre Steinlen

051. Alphonse Maria Mucha

054. ETHEL REED

053. EUGÈNE GRASSET

056. Jules-Alexandre Grün

055. Jules Chéret

058. JULES CHÉRET

057. PRIVAT LIVEMONT

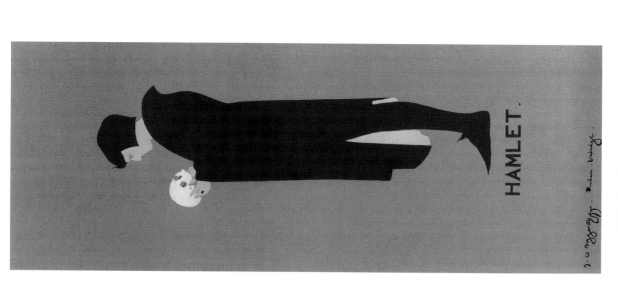

059. THE BEGGARSTAFFS

060. JULES CHÉRET

062. Maurice Réalier-Dumas

061. Henri de Toulouse-Lautrec

064. Edward Penfield

063. Alphonse Maria Mucha

066. FRED HYLAND

065. FÉLIX VALLOTTON

068. HENRI DE TOULOUSE-LAUTREC

067. JULES CHÉRET

070. FRITZ REHM

069. MAXFIELD PARRISH

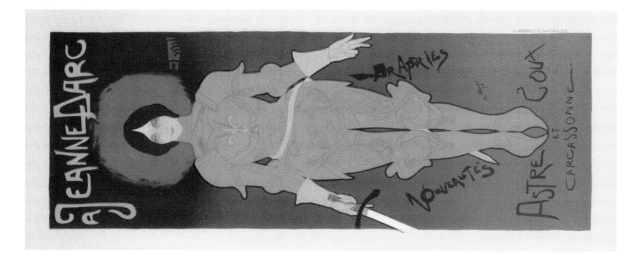

072. GEORGES DE FEURE

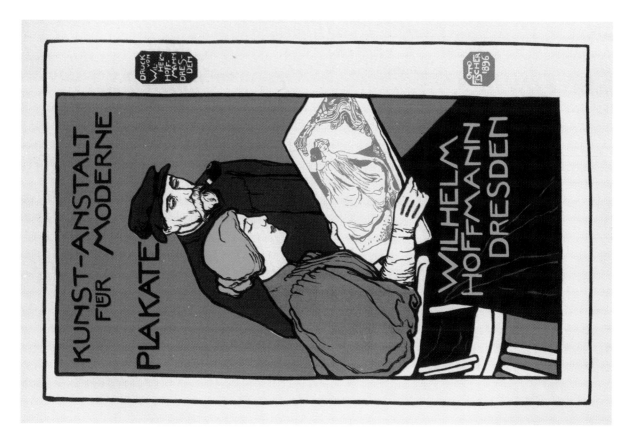

071. OTTO FISCHER

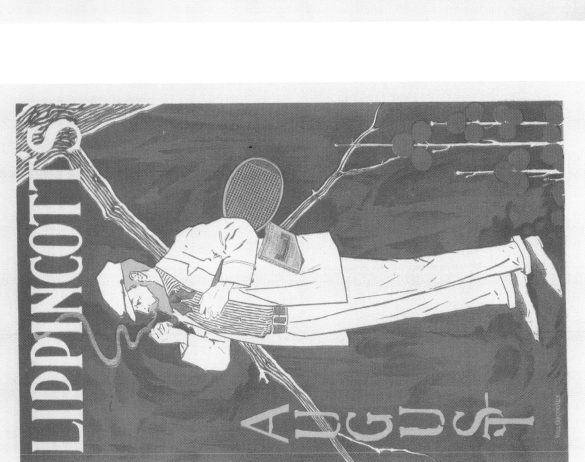

074. MANUEL ROBBE

073. WILLIAM CARQUEVILLE

076. Jules Chéret

075. Alphonse Maria Mucha

078. JULES CHÉRET

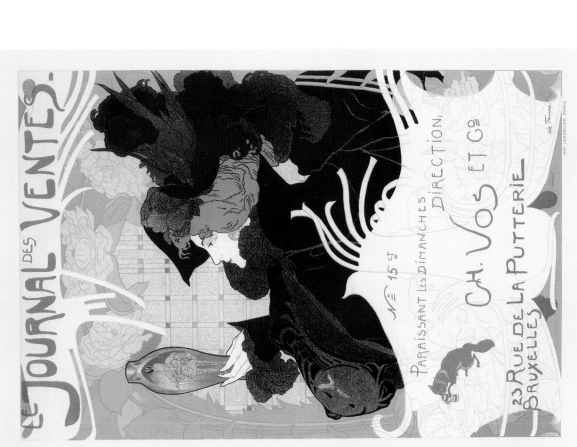

077. GEORGES DE FEURE

079. Louis Anquetin

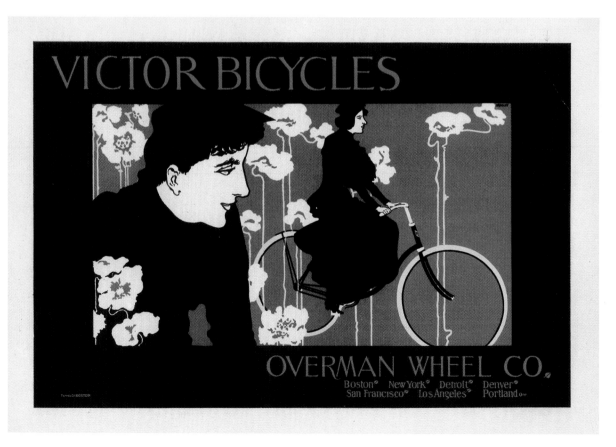

080. Will Bradley

082. Etienne Moreau-Nélaton

081 Eugène Grasset

084. THE BEGGARSTAFFS

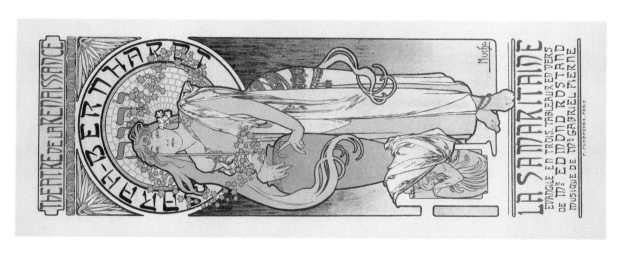

083. ALPHONSE MARIA MUCHA

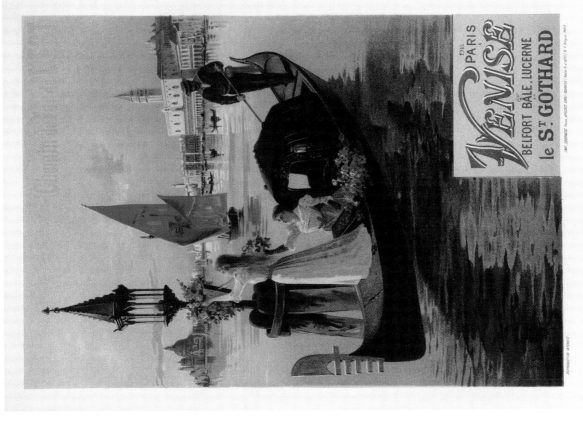

086. F. HUGO D'ALÉSI

085. THÉOPHILE-ALEXANDRE STEINLEN

088. Eugène Grasset

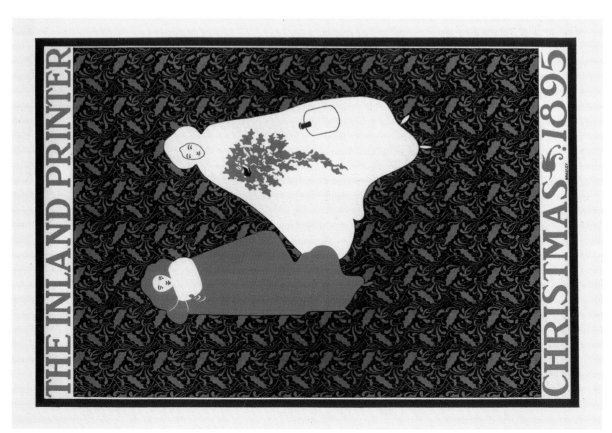

087. Will Bradley

090. JULES CHÉRET

089. VÁCLAV OLIVA

092. Alphonse Maria Mucha

091. Adolph Hohenstein

094. JULES CHÉRET

093. THE BEGGARSTAFFS

096. RENÉ PÉAN

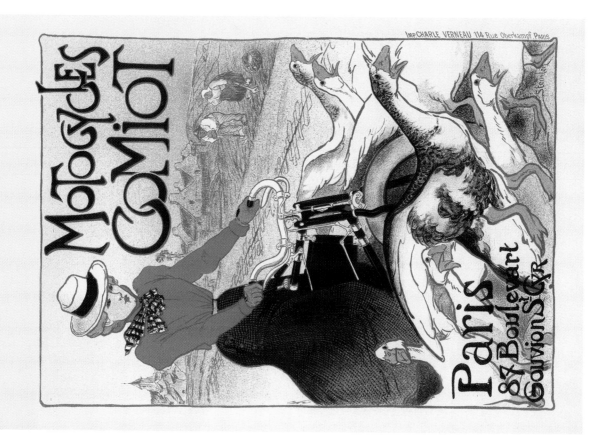

095. THÉOPHILE-ALEXANDRE STEINLEN

098. HENRI MEUNIER

097. G. BOANO

100. ALPHONSE MARIA MUCHA

099. LOUIS RHEAD

101. Fernel (F. Cerckel)

102. Jules Chéret

104. JULES CHÉRET

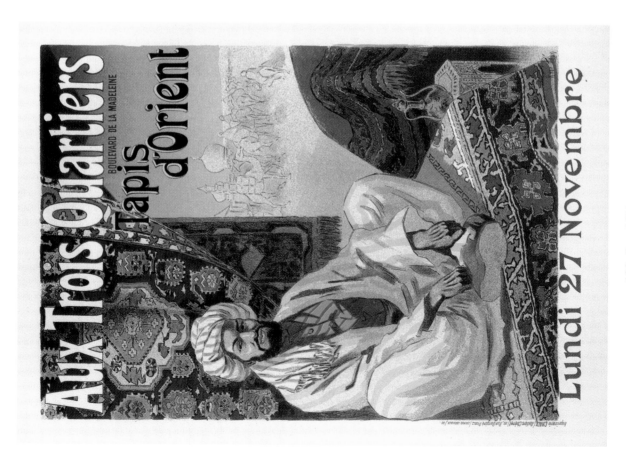

103. RENÉ PÉAN

106. JULES CHÉRET

105. DUDLEY HARDY

107. Louis Rhead

108. Henri Meunier

110. H. Thomas

109. Fernand Gottlob

112. Paul Berthon

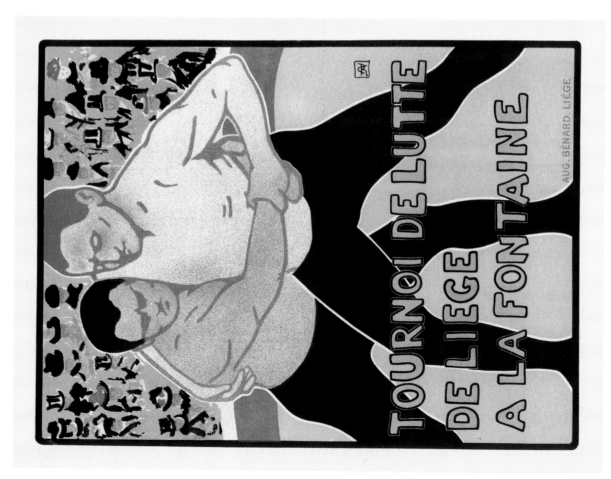

111. Armand Rassenfosse

THÉÂTRE NATIONAL DE L'OPÉRA COMIQUE

LOUISE de Gustave Charpentier

roman musical en 5 actes et 4 tableaux

G.Rochegrosse

Publié avec l'autorisation de M.M. HEUGEL et Cie. "AU MÉNESTREL" 2, BIS, RUE VIVIENNE, ÉDITEURS PROPRIÉTAIRES

Paris: Ed.DELANCHY & Cie 51 & 53, Faub.9 St-Denis.

114. GEORGES ROCHEGROSSE

Red Star Line

Anvers New York

AFFICHES D'ART O.DE RYCKER BRUXELLES 18982

113. HENDRICK CASSIERS

116. REISNER

115. THE BEGGARSTAFFS

117. Georges Fay

118. Henri Toulouse-Lautrec

120. Van Caspel

119. Fernand Gottlob

List of Plates

The entries in this list give the following information in the following order: artist's name; original date; dimensions of original poster, height before width, in centimeters and in inches (rounded off to whole and half-inches); and a full translation of the poster text (if not already in English), with additional explanations in square brackets wherever necessary.

001. JULES CHÉRET; 1895; 124×88 cm (49×34.5 in). Text: "Job cigarette paper; [judged] above competition [at the World's Fair], Paris, 1889."

002. HENRI DE TOULOUSE-LAUTREC; 1892; 81×62 cm (32×24.5 in). Text: "Divan Japonais [music hall], 75 rue des Martyrs; Ed. Fournier, director."

003. JULIUS PRICE; 1895; 216×150 cm (85.5×59 in). [Musical comedy ad.]

004. DUDLEY HARDY; 1894; 76×50 cm (30×20 in). [Musical comedy ad.]

005. GEORGES MEUNIER; 1895; 246×88 cm (97×34.5 in).

006. LOUIS RHEAD; 1894; 116×76 cm (45.5×30 in). [Newspaper ad.]

007. JULES CHÉRET; 1896; 124×88 cm (49×34.5 in). Text: "Théâtre de l'Opéra, 1896 Carnival, on the Saturday before Lent, February 15, gala fancy-dress ball."

008. GEORGES DE FEURE; 1894; 64×43 cm (25×17 in). Text: "Fifth exhibition, October 1–31, Salon des Cent, 31 rue Bonaparte; admission 50 centimes."

009. LUCIEN LEFÈVRE; 1893; 124×88 cm (49×34.5 in). Text: "Charles Gravier's chocolate milk, better than all known chocolates and cocoas, 6 francs per kilo; main store, 44 rue de Louvre, Paris, and available at every pharmacy and grocery."

010. F.-A. CAZALS; 1894; 61×40 cm (24×16 in). Text: "Seventh exhibition of the Salon des Cent, 31 rue Bonaparte, December 1894; admission 1 franc." [Depicted are the poets Paul Verlaine and Jean Moréas.]

011. THE BEGGARSTAFFS; 1895; 220×200 cm (86.5×79 in).

012. JULES CHÉRET; 1896; 124×88 cm (49×34.5 in). Text: "Ice Palace, Champs-Elysées."

013. EUGÈNE GRASSET; 1891; 140×84 cm (55×33 in). Text: "A la Place Clichy, world's finest establishment for Oriental imports."

014. EDWARD PENFIELD; 1894; 49×35 cm (19.5×14 in).

015. LUCIEN MÉTIVET; 1893; 118×80 cm (42.5×31.5 in). Text: "Nightly, Eugénie Buffet, Ambassadeurs [music hall]."

016. MAURICE GREIFFENHAGEN; 1894; 200×150 cm (79×59 in).

017. MAURICE BOUTET DE MONVEL; 1894; 82×61 cm (32×22.5 in). Text: "Toothpaste of Dr. Pierre of the Paris faculty of medicine; for sale everywhere."

018. ALPHONSE MARIA MUCHA; 1894; 211×69 cm (83×27 in). Text: "Gismonda, Sarah Bernhardt, Théâtre de la Renaissance."

019. EDOUARD DUYCK and ADOLPHE CRESPIN; 1894; 118×89 cm (42.5×35 in). Text: "Spa, Frahinfaz Farm, café and restaurant, Sart hippodrome road; knife-and-fork lunch, fresh milk [from?] Chefnaie, real Brussels Faro [beer?], English beers; lodging for arrivals on foot or on horseback."

020. ALBERT GUILLAUME; 1894; 190×125 cm (75×49 in). Text: "Ambigue-Comique [theater], Gigolette."

021. JULES CHÉRET; 1890; 124×88 cm (49×34.5 in). Text: "Théâtrophone [phone hookup to theatrical performances]."

022. PIERRE BONNARD; 1894; 80×62 cm (31.5×24.5 in). Text: "The Revue Blanche [magazine] is published every month in issues of 100 pages, 1 franc per copy; offices at 1 rue Laffitte; for sale everywhere."

023. GASTON NOURY; 1892; 139×99 cm (54.5×39 in). Text: "For the poor of France and Russia; grand festival at the Tuileries, August 13–21; main office, 63 boulevard St-Michel; see the special poster for the program."

024. JULES CHÉRET; 1892; 124×88 cm (49×34.5 in). Text: "Musée Grévin, Pantomimes of Light, E[mile] Reynaud's Optical Theater; music by Gaston Paulin; daily from 3 to 6 and from 8 to 11."

025. ADOLPHE WILLETTE; 1893; 193×67 cm (76×26.5 in). Text: "Have some Van Houten cocoa."

026. WILLIAM CARQUEVILLE; 1895; 48×31.5 cm (19×12.5 in). [Magazine ad.]

027. FIRMIN BOUISSET; 1893; 130×94 cm (51×37 in). Text: "Menier chocolate."

028. WILL BRADLEY; 1890; 44×36 cm (17.5×14 in). [Ad for book of verse.]

029. JULES CHÉRET; 1889; 124×88 cm (49×34.5 in). Text: "Dancing at the Moulin Rouge, place Blanche [Montmartre]; every night and Sunday matinée; grand festival on Wednesdays and Saturdays."

030. LUCIEN LEFÈVRE; 1895; 124×88 cm (49×34.5 in). Text: "Electricine, luxury lighting."

031. GEORGES MEUNIER; 1895; 124×88 cm (49×34.5 in). text: "Grand garden of the Elysée Montmartre; every night, Trianon-Concert; 80 boulevard Rochechouart; varsity show."

032. THE BEGGARSTAFFS; 1896; 213×198 cm (84×78 in). [Play ad.]

033. JOSEPH SATTLER; 1895; 35×28 cm (14×11 in). Text: "Pan [magazine], 1895–96."

034. CARAN D'ACHE; 1895; 139×90 cm (55×35.5 in). Text: "Russian exhibition; Champ-de-Mars [, Paris]."

035. JULES CHÉRET; 1893; 124×88 cm (49×34.5 in); green and red state. Text: "Folies-Bergère, Loie Fuller."

036. ROEDEL; 1896; 130×91 cm (51×36 in). Text: "Moulin de la Galette; founded 1295; matinee dancing, Sundays and holidays; grand sports garden; wonderful view."

037. M. LOUISE STOWELL; 1896; 64×43 cm (25×17 in).

038. HENRI-GABRIEL IBELS; 1895; 168×120 cm (66×47 in). Text: "Mévisto [an entertainer]."

039. ALBERT GEORGE MORROW; 1894; 62×47 cm (24.5×18.5 in).

040. HENRI DE TOULOUSE-LAUTREC; 1895; 128×93 cm (51×36.5 in). Text: "The Revue Blanche, bimonthly; 60 centimes a copy, 12 francs a year; 1 rue Lafitte, Paris; published by Charpentier & Fasquelle, 11 rue de Grenelle."

041. HENRI GERBAULT; ca. 1895; 130×95 cm (51×37.5 in). Text: "Carpentier chocolate."

042. PAUL FISCHER; ca. 1895; 82×60 cm (32×23.5 in). Text: "Vilhelm Søborg's successors; advertising posters; artistic assistance; 36 Fiolstræde."

043. JULES CHÉRET; 1894; 124×75 cm (49×29.5 in). Text: "Winter 1894–1895; Wednesday, January 16; students' ball [at the] Closerie des Lilas (Bullier ballroom); tickets at the office of the Students' Association, 41 rue des Ecoles."

044. MISTI; 1895; 148×100 cm (58×39.5 in). Text: "Gladiator bicycles, boulevard Montmartre."

045. OTTO FISCHER; 1896; 69×102 cm (27×40 in). Text: "Exhibition of Saxon artisanry and commercial art, Dresden, 1896; the old city."

046. PRIVAT LIVEMONT; 1896; 75×110 cm (29.5×43 in). Text: "Cabourg, 5 hours from Paris."

047. LUCIEN LEFÈVRE; 1894; 176×124 cm (69×49 in). Text: "Jacquot & Co. shoe polish; General Society of French Shoe Polishes, Paris."

048. ADOLPHE CRESPIN; ca. 1896; 54×40 cm (21×16 in). Text: "Paul Hankar, architect, rue Defacqz 63."

049. DUDLEY HARDY; ca. 1895; 295×195 cm (116×76.5 in).

050. JULES CHÉRET; 1896; 124×88 cm (49×34.5 in). Text: "Camille Stéfani."

051. ALPHONSE MARIA MUCHA; 1896; 64×43 cm (25×17 in). Text: "20th exhibition of the Salon des Cent (March–April 1896); entrance hall of La Plume [(editorial offices of the magazine) The Pen], 31 rue Bonaparte, Paris; admission 50 centimes."

052. THÉOPHILE-ALEXANDRE STEINLEN; 1894; 140×100 cm (55×39.5 in). Text: "Sterilized pure milk from the Vingeanne, Guillot Brothers, Montigny sur Vingeanne, Côte d'Or [Burgundy]."

053. EUGÈNE GRASSET; 1894; 61×41 cm (24×16 in). Text: "Salon des Cent, 31 rue Bonaparte, Paris (April 5–25); 5 francs on Tuesdays, 1 franc other days, free on Sundays; exhibition of a part of the works of E. Grasset."

054. ETHEL REED; 1895; 56×35 cm (22×14 in).

055. JULES CHÉRET; 1890; 124×88 cm (49×34.5 in). Text: "Bagnères-de-Luchon [in the Pyrenees] flower festival, Sunday, August 10."

056. JULES-ALEXANDRE GRÜN; 1897; 126×92 cm (49.5×36 in). Text: "Where are they taking her? 'To the Hoosegow'; evenings at 9, Café Riche, boulevard des Italiens."

057. PRIVAT LIVEMONT; 1896; 111×83 cm (43.5×32.5 in). Text: "Robette absinthe."

058. JULES CHÉRET; 1897; 124×88 cm (49×34.5 in). Text: "Théâtre de l'Opéra; Saturday, January 22; grand party at the Opera; first masked ball."

059. THE BEGGARSTAFFS; stenciled poster, 1894; 180×75 cm (71×29.5 in).

060. JULES CHÉRET; 1895; 124×88 cm (49×34.5 in). Text: "Dubonnet quinine-flavored apéritif, at all cafés."

061. HENRI DE TOULOUSE-LAUTREC; 1893; 130×94 cm (51×37 in). Text: "Jane Avril [at the music hall] Jardin de Paris."

062. MAURICE RÉALIER-DUMAS; 1895; 176×62 cm (69.5×24.5 in). Text: "Jules Mumm & Co. champagne, Reims."

063. ALPHONSE MARIA MUCHA; 1896; 207×77 cm (81.5×30.5 in). Text: "Lorenzaccio, a play in five acts and an epilogue by Alfred de Musset, adapted by Mr. Armand d'Artois; Sarah Bernhardt, A.D. 1896; Théâtre de la Renaissance."

064. EDWARD PENFIELD; 1897; 45×30 cm (18×12 in). [Magazine ad.]

065. FÉLIX VALLOTTON; ca. 1895; 129×93 cm (51×36.5 in). Text: "Ah! la Pé . . . la Pé . . . la Pépinière!!!," revue in two acts and four scenes by Albert Pajol and Adolphe Couturet; new melodies, adapted music and ballet by Jacoutot; costumes designed by Japhet and executed by Louise Caffard; sets by Ménessier; cast: [listing of the actors and their numerous roles]; nightly at 9:30; Sunday and holiday matinées at 2; Concert de la Pépinière [(Tree) Nursery] (near the St-Lazare station).

066. FRED HYLAND; 1896; 75×50 cm (29.5×19.5 in).

067. JULES CHÉRET; 1890; 124×88 cm (49×34.5 in). Text: "La Diaphane, Sarah Bernhardt rice powder; 32 avenue de l'Opéra, Paris."

068. HENRI DE TOULOUSE-LAUTREC; 1891; 170×120 cm (67×47 in). Text: "Moulin Rouge; dance nightly; La Goulue [the Glutton]."

069. MAXFIELD PARRISH; 1897; 51×34 cm (20×13.5 in).

070. FRITZ REHM; 1897; 88×58 cm (34.5×23 in). Text: "The connoisseur; Laferme cigarettes, Dresden; award-winning original from the poster competition of the art printers Grimme & Hempel Co., Leipzig."

071. OTTO FISCHER; 1896; 95×64 cm (37.5×25 in). Text: "Printers of modern posters; Wilhelm Hoffmann, Dresden."

072. GEORGES DE FEURE; 1896; 243×93 cm (95.5×36.5 in). Text: "At the Sign of Joan of Arc; fancy goods, dry goods; Astre and Goux, Carcassonne."

073. WILLIAM CARQUEVILLE; 1895; 48×31 cm (19×12 in). [Magazine ad.]

074. MANUEL ROBBE; 1895; 130×94 cm (51×37 in). Text: "L'Eclatante [the brilliant (lamp)], wickless kerosene lamp; 36 & 38, rue de Chabrol."

075. ALPHONSE MARIA MUCHA; 1896; 207×77 cm (81.5×30.5 in). Text: "La dame aux camélias ["Camille"]; Sarah Bernhardt; Théâtre de la Renaissance."

076. JULES CHÉRET; 1892; 124×88 cm (49×34.5 in). Text: "Saxoléine safety kerosene; extra-white, odorless, nonin-flammable; in 5-liter leaded cans."

077. GEORGES DE FEURE; 1897; 65×50 cm (25.5×20 in). Text: "Journal des Ventes [Auction Record], 15 centimes a copy; comes out on Sundays; published by Ch. Vos ["fox" in Flemish, hence the logo] and Co., 23 rue de la Putterie, Brussels."

078. JULES CHÉRET; 1898; 124×88 cm (49×34.5 in). Text: "Théâtre de l'Opéra; Saturday, January 7 [1899]; grand fes-tivities; first masked ball."

079. LOUIS ANQUETIN; ca. 1894; 128×94 cm (37×50.5 in). Text: "Marguerite Dufay performing her specialties."

080. WILL BRADLEY; 1896; 68×104 cm (27×41 in).

081 EUGÈNE GRASSET; 1892; 117×76 cm (46×30 in). Text: "L. Marquet ink, the best ink of all."

082. ETIENNE MOREAU-NÉLATON; 1897; 134×95 cm (53×37.5 in). Text: "Palace of Fine Arts, Champ de Mars [, Paris], from May 15 to July 31, 1897, national exhibition of ceramics and all arts of the kiln."

083. ALPHONSE MARIA MUCHA; 1897; 169×54 cm (66.5×21 in). Text: "Théâtre de la Renaissance; Sarah Bernhardt; [in Hebrew; "Jehovah"]; *The Woman of Samaria,* verse gospel play in three scenes by Mr. Edmond Rostand, music by Mr. Gabriel Pierné."

084. THE BEGGARSTAFFS; 1895; 95×70 cm (37.5×27.5 in).

085. THÉOPHILE-ALEXANDRE STEINLEN; 1896; 76×55 cm (30×21.5 in). Text: "French Chocolate and Tea Company."

086. F. HUGO D'ALÉSI; ca. 1890; 102×62 cm (40×24.5 in). Text: "Eastern railroad line; from Paris to Venice via Belfort, Basel, Lucerne and the St. Gotthard pass."

087. WILL BRADLEY; 1895; 44×36 cm (17.5×14 in). [Magazine ad.]

088. EUGÈNE GRASSET; 1893; 114×70 cm (45×27.5 in). Text: "*Joan of Arc* [with] Sarah Bernhardt [at the Théâtre de la Renaissance]."

089. VÁCLAV OLIVA; ca. 1898; 100×35 cm (39.5×14 in). Text: "Order the splendid illustrated weekly *Golden Prague;* quarterly 2 gulden, by mail 2. 38, single copies 33 kreutzers; editorial office of *Golden Prague,* 34 Karel Place, Otto's Book Printing Establishment; at every bookdealer's."

090. JULES CHÉRET; 1887; 250×96 cm (98.5×38 in).

091. ADOLPH HOHENSTEIN; 1898; 120×65 cm (47×25.5 in) [*sic*]. Text: "*Iris* [an opera], music by P[ietro] Mascagni, libretto by L[uigi] Illica, published by G. Ricordi & Co."

092. ALPHONSE MARIA MUCHA; 1898; 139×88 cm (55×34.5 in). Text: "Beers of the Meuse [département]; Bar-le-Duc [city]; at the Caves [cellars] du Roy, Sèvres."

093. THE BEGGARSTAFFS; 1895; 295×195 cm (116×76.5 in). [*A Trip to Chinatown* was an American musical comedy.]

094. JULES CHÉRET; 1890; 235×80 cm (90.5×31.5 in). Text: "Grands Magasins du Louvre [a department store]; toys, New Year's gifts, 1891."

095. THÉOPHILE-ALEXANDRE STEINLEN; 1899; 133×92 cm (52.5×36 in). Text: "Comiot motorcycles, Paris, 87 boulevard Gouvion, St-Cyr."

096. RENÉ PÉAN; 1898; 124×88 cm (49×34.5 in). Text: "A la Place Clichy [store]; Monday, March 7, novelties of the season, distribution of bouquets from Nice."

097. G. BOANO; 1898; 121×84 cm (47.5×33 in). Text: "Royal Theater [opera house], Turin."

098. HENRI MEUNIER; 1899; 82×40 cm (32×16 in). Text: "Starlight soap."

099. LOUIS RHEAD; 1896; 118×73 cm (46.5×29 in). [Newspaper ad.]

100. ALPHONSE MARIA MUCHA; 1898; 51×39 cm (20×15.5 in). Text: "Job [cigarette paper]."

101. FERNEL (F. CERCKEL); 1899; 118×84 cm (46.5×33 in). Text: "Grand Bazar des Halles et des Postes [a store]; toys, New Year's gifts; rues du Louvre, Coquillière and du Bouloi [, Paris]."

102. JULES CHÉRET; 1889; 170×115 cm (67×45 in). Text: "For sale everywhere, *Le rappel* [The Recall to the Colors; a newspaper], 5 centimes a copy."

103. RENÉ PÉAN; 1899; 150×100 cm (59×39.5 in). Text: "Aux Trois Quartiers [At the Three Quarters; a store], boulevard de la Madeleine [, Paris]; Oriental carpets; Monday, November 27."

104. JULES CHÉRET; 1899; 105×81 cm (41.5×32 in). Text: "Pippermint; Get Bros., in Revel (Haute Garonne [département]); at all cafés, wine dealers, groceries."

105. DUDLEY HARDY; ca. 1895; 295×195 cm (116×76.5 in).

106. JULES CHÉRET; 1899; 119×81 cm (46.5×32 in). Text: "Olympia Tavern; restaurant open all night; women's orchestra; roller coaster; 28 boulevard des Capucines & 6 rue Caumartin [, Paris]."

107. LOUIS RHEAD; 1895; 115×145 cm (17.5×45 in).

108. HENRI MEUNIER; 1897; 56×71 cm (22×28 in). [Coffee ad.]

109. FERNAND GOTTLOB; 1899; 112×74 cm (44×29 in). Text: "2nd exhibition of painter-lithographers, January 10–25, public hall of *Le Figaro* [newspaper], rue Drouot [, Paris]."

110. H. THOMAS; 1897; 125×90 cm (49×35.5 in). Text: "L'Eclair [The Lightning Flash]; 5 centimes; independent political newspaper; first prize in *L'Eclair*'s poster competition."

111. ARMAND RASSENFOSSE; 1899; 100×74 cm (39.5×29 in). Text: "Wrestling tournament of Liège at La Fontaine."

112. PAUL BERTHON; 1897; 44×62 cm (24.5×17.5 in). Text: "*L'ermitage* [The Hermitage], illustrated magazine, 8 francs a year; 18 rue de l'Odéon, Paris."

113. HENDRICK CASSIERS; 1899; 86×58 cm (34×23 in). Text: "Red Star Line, Antwerp/New York."

114. GEORGES ROCHEGROSSE; 1900; 80×60 cm (31.5×23.5 in). Text: "National Opéra-Comique Theater; *Louise,* a novel in music [opera], in 4 acts and 5 scenes, by Gustave Charpentier; published by permission of Heugel & Co., "At the Sign of the Minstrel," 2 *bis* rue Vivienne [, Paris], publishers and proprietors."

115. THE BEGGARSTAFFS; 1894; 143×95 cm (56.5×37.5 in).

116. REISNER; 1898; 95×63 cm (37.5×25 in). Text: "Jewelry and silverware shop, producing its own items; F. & D. Malý, Prague, I. Postovská VI. 4; large assortment of fashionable novelties."

117. GEORGES FAY; 1900; 110×150 cm (43.5×59 in). Text: "Central Agricultural Association of France, 19 rue Louis-le-Grand, Paris."

118. HENRI TOULOUSE-LAUTREC; 1896; 80×118 cm (31.5×46.5 in). Text: "The Simpson bicycle chain; L. B. Spoke, manager for France; 25 boulevard Haussmann [, Paris]."

119. FERNAND GOTTLOB; 1898; 55×36 cm (21.5×14 in). Text: "December 1–31; Salon des Cent, 31 rue Bonaparte [, Paris]; studies by F. Gottlob."

120. VAN CASPEL; ca. 1898; 70×47 cm (27.5×18.5 in). Text: "W. Hoogenstraaten & Co.; fine vegetables, cooking greens, soups and sauces."

Alphabetical List of Artists